www.providencebooks.net

Publisher Contact

Email:contact@providencebooks.net

Social media: facebook.com/providencebooks

Acknowledgements

The team at Providence Books would like to thank our friends, family, suppliers and customers for making our vision of creating the highest-quality books a reality. Thanks for purchasing and enjoy the quotes!

This page is intentionally left blank

This page is intentionally left blank

A corporation's responsibility is to the shareholders, not its retirees and employees. Companies are doing everything they can to get rid of pension plans and they will succeed.

Ben Stein

Academic freedom is being lost by a great many people who dare to challenge Darwinism. That's a terrifying situation. That's contrary to the principles of science.

Ben Stein

After all the black man has been through in this world, he can still often reach levels of spirituality the most pampered white man cannot touch. Maybe what he's been through is the reason why.

Ben Stein

Americans are terrified because so many of them have been laid off in recent years and months and they fear that they may be next. Even if they have not been laid off or have not known anyone laid off, they definitely know someone who has lost his home.

Ben Stein

As Beverly Hills becomes more Iranian-Jewish, it is becoming politically conservative.

Ben Stein

As to a media personality, well that just happened in large measure because people found me amusing, and I did lots and lots of T.V. news interview shows.

Ben Stein

Darwinism doesn't explain where gravity comes from. It doesn't explain where thermodynamics comes from. It doesn't explain where the laws of physics come from. It doesn't explain where matter came from.

Ben Stein

Emperor Sid Caesar is gone to eternity himself now. He takes with him the gratitude of every one of us who first learned the relief of laughter from this genuinely great performer.

Ben Stein

Every soul deserves a shot at a Cadillac, but not everyone should be guaranteed a Cadillac.

Ben Stein

Faith is not believing that God can. It is knowing that God will.

Ben Stein

For me, I've always believed that there was a God. I've always believed that God created the heavens and earth - so, for me it's not a huge leap from there to intelligent design.

Ben Stein

Greed is a basic part of animal nature. Being against it is like being against breathing or eating. It means nothing.

Ben Stein

Hollywood is largely about scammers and con men. It was my main livelihood for about 25 years, and the scams were beautiful and ugly, cheap and expensive, but, wow, were there a lot of scammers.

Ben Stein

I agree that there are some bad apples on Wall Street. I spent about ten years exposing corporate and financial fraud for 'Barron's' magazine and I found a lot to write about.

Ben Stein

I always assumed scientists were free to ask any question, pursue any line of inquiry without fear or reprisal.

Ben Stein

I am a Jew, and every single one of my ancestors was Jewish. And it does not bother me even a little bit when people call those beautiful lit up, bejeweled trees Christmas trees. I don't feel threatened. I don't feel discriminated against.

Ben Stein

I am about to vote. I am about to do something that human beings are rarely allowed to do. I am doing something that did not exist until America.

Ben Stein

I am scared of getting old. I am scared of being ill.

Ben Stein

I am scared of running out of money.

Ben Stein

I am so in love with just lying in bed listening to Mozart.

Ben Stein

I am so used to having a comfortable life. What will it be like when I am no longer able to just buy anything I want?

Ben Stein

I do all of the grocery shopping in my little family. I buy cheese, of many different kinds, sliced packaged meats and poultry, bagels, immense quantities of eggs, pre-made fried chicken. Milk. Bacon. It is insane how much dairy, deli and bakery stuff I buy.

Ben Stein

I don't believe the most successful people are the ones who got the best grades, got into the best schools, or made the most money.

Ben Stein

I don't like getting pushed around for being a Jew, and I don't think Christians like getting pushed around for being Christians. I think people who believe in God are sick and tired of getting pushed around, period.

Ben Stein

I don't like the sound of all the lists he's making.

Ben Stein

I don't really consider myself to be a personal finance expert compared with some others. There are quite a few that know a lot more than I do.

Ben Stein

I have a great pic of my father and Rev. Graham laughing hysterically at some joke with George Pratt Shultz looking on back in 1972 or so.

Ben Stein

I have always been very concerned that Darwinism gave the basic okay to terrible racism and to the idea of murder based upon race.

Ben Stein

I have no idea where the concept came from that America is an explicitly atheist country. I can't find it in the Constitution, and I don't like it being shoved down my throat.

Ben Stein

I have to tell you I never in my life anticipated getting this old, this fast. It seems as if I were 25 just a few days ago.

Ben Stein

I love sleeping in a moving car more than sleeping in bed.

Ben Stein

I spend so much time in fear of going broke, and I never have been even remotely close to going broke.

Ben Stein

I tell you why I don't think I will ever vote for a Democrat, if I may say so. Because for me, the number one issue is right to life, and I don't think the Democrats are very good on the right-to-life issue.

Ben Stein

I think Darwinism as a theory explaining evolution within species is incredibly brilliant - just unbelievably, incredibly brilliant.

Ben Stein

I think it's criminal how little people in the military are paid. These are people out risking their lives, taken away from their families for long periods of time. I think they should be paid dramatically more than they're paid.

Ben Stein

I thought that all of the sacrifices and blessings of the whole history of mankind have devolved upon me. Thank you, God.

Ben Stein

I was a trial lawyer. At the same time, I was a teacher. I taught about the political and social content of film for American University. Then I left and became a teacher at the University of California at Santa Cruz. I taught about the political and social content of film, but I also taught a course in law for undergraduates.

Ben Stein

I'd say the main way people get into terrible financial trouble is just to spend too much money relative to their income, and that is an endemic problem in the United States of America, and that's the kind of thing that should be taught about in schools.

Ben Stein

I'm an economist by training. I don't really work as an economist. I only worked briefly as an economist.

Ben Stein

I'm not a Mensa member. I have no idea where that rumor came from. I never have been, and I doubt if I ever will be.

Ben Stein

If Iran and North Korea, by some horrible, devilish, nightmarish scenario, got together and went to war at the same time, one against Saudi Arabia and one against South Korea, I don't know what we would do about that. I don't know that we could stop them short of using nuclear weapons.

Ben Stein

If there are finer beings than German short hairs, I don't know what they are. In their eyes is peace.

Ben Stein

If there is no God, then man sometimes thinks he is god, and sometimes tries to live like a god.

Ben Stein

If there is no God, why bother to tell the truth? Why not steal?

Ben Stein

If there's a recession, I'd buy stocks. That's when you make money: when markets are spooked.

Ben Stein

If we are just specks of dust hit by lightning, if we have no spark of God in us, why not just take whatever we can and devil take the hindmost? I mean, we are fools not to do that if there is no right or wrong.

Ben Stein

If we try to engineer outcomes, if we overturn tradition to make everyone the same, we ruin society. If we upset tradition to allow for an equal shot at the starting gate, everyone wins, except for the charlatans and would be dictators.

Ben Stein

If you can't stand the heat, don't go to Cancun in the summer.

Ben Stein

If you want to fight the evil you see in finance and industry, get to work reading the corporate filings, see if there has been fraud, and where you find it, report it to the SEC or write about it or blog about it.

Ben Stein

Israel being condemned by the EU, which 66 years ago watched with glee as its Jews were being mass murdered. That is pretty rich.

Ben Stein

Israel is our strongest, most reliable ally in the Middle East. Of course, we're their most reliable ally, too.

Ben Stein

It doesn't bother me a bit when people say, 'Merry Christmas' to me. I don't think they are slighting me or getting ready to put me in a ghetto. In fact, I kind of like it.

Ben Stein

It is inevitable that some defeat will enter even the most victorious life. The human spirit is never finished when it is defeated... it is finished when it surrenders.

Ben Stein

It is so great to sleep in safe, glorious, beautiful America. I just cannot get over it.

Ben Stein

It isn't the rich people's fault that poor people are poor. Poor people who get an education and work hard in this country will stop being poor. That should be the goal for all poor people everywhere.

Ben Stein

It means zero to be against greed.

Ben Stein

It's a great stretch for me to do my game show. It's very hard. It's not me at all. The only part that's me is sort of when I'm sitting in the booth looking tormented. That's the only part that's the real me.

Ben Stein

It's amazing what ordinary people can do if they set out without preconceived notions.

Ben Stein

It's really amazing that in the age of unbelief, as a smart man called it, there isn't even more fraud. After all, with no God, there's no one to ever call you to account, and no accounting at all if you can get away with it.

Ben Stein

Jump into the middle of things, get your hands dirty, fall flat on your face, and then reach for the stars.

Ben Stein

Keep on beginning and failing. Each time you fail, start all over gain, and you will grow stronger until have accomplished a purpose - not the one you began with perhaps, but one you'll be glad to remember.

Ben Stein

Men and women succeed because they find a field of endeavor that matches their interests and abilities.

Ben Stein

My 'thing' is that I just lie in my immense bed and look out the window at the skyline over Virginia and the sky and the airplanes coming into Reagan. I really love doing that.

Ben Stein

My pals, such as they are, in Hollywood, ask me why I love to travel to D.C. so much, why it's a vacation destination for me. I say, 'Because I sometimes have perfect days there.'

Ben Stein

My parents, products of the Great Depression, were successful people, but lived in a state of constant fear that my sister and I, and they, would sink into the kind of economic insecurity that their generation knew so well.

Ben Stein

Nothing happens by itself... it all will come your way, once you understand that you have to make it come your way, by your own exertions.

Ben Stein

Now, although my life is still pleasant, the days of easy money are over.

Ben Stein

People ask how I can be a conservative and still want higher taxes. It makes my head spin, and I guess it shows how old I am. But I thought that conservatives were supposed to like balanced budgets. I thought it was the conservative position to not leave heavy indebtedness to our grandchildren.

Ben Stein

People getting rich in a free society in general - with some scammy exceptions, which are rare - makes everyone else richer, too.

Ben Stein

Personal relationships are the fertile soil from which all advancement, all success, all achievement in real life grows.

Ben Stein

Put simply, the rich pay a lot of taxes as a total percentage of taxes collected, but they don't pay a lot of taxes as a percentage of what they can afford to pay, or as a percentage of what the government needs to close the deficit gap.

Ben Stein

Running a real business is exacting, daunting, repetitive work. Even in Silicon Valley.

Ben Stein

Science should always be in the business of attempting to disprove itself.

Ben Stein

Screaming at children over their grades, especially to the point of the child's tears, is child abuse, pure and simple. It's not funny and it's not good parenting. It is a crushing, scarring, disastrous experience for the child. It isn't the least bit funny.

Ben Stein

Sleep makes people calmer, more alert, less fearful - just plain happier, or so I see around me and in me. I am sure that if this great nation were to concentrate on getting more sleep, we would be a happier, more confident people, and that by itself would be a major achievement.

Ben Stein

Sleep more at night. If it's allowed at work or home, take a nap in the afternoon. You'll be amazed at how much better you'll feel.

Ben Stein

So many fail because they don't get started - they don't go. They don't overcome inertia. They don't begin.

Ben Stein

So, who in the media is without sin among us? I am in the media and I am a major league sinner. I don't know anyone except my wife who isn't a big time sinner.

Ben Stein

Somewhere there is a map of how it can be done.

Ben Stein

The America that we knew as the smartest place on the planet is gone with the wind.

Ben Stein

The banks are not lending, at least from what I see. They were so wild and reckless back in the good times that they got burned terribly.

Ben Stein

The education system should teach us about money; it's an incredibly big subject. I run into people all the time that don't have the first clue of what they should do about money.

Ben Stein

The first step to getting the things you want out of life is this: Decide what you want.

Ben Stein

The human spirit needs to accomplish, to achieve, to triumph to be happy.

Ben Stein

The indispensable first step to getting the things you want out of life is this: decide what you want.

Ben Stein

The ordinary American - as far as I can tell - knows so much less than he did fifty years ago and has such poor work habits compared with fifty years ago that the average multiplicand of knowledge/capabilities is a much smaller number than it was in 1961.

Ben Stein

The people who did the collateralized mortgage obligations, sold them to pension funds, then sold them short, then bought credit default swap insurance on them, are just amazing. They are a law unto themselves.

Ben Stein

The sad fact is that spending rises every year, no matter what people want or say they want.

Ben Stein

The successful people of this world take life as it comes. They just go out and deal with the world as it is.

Ben Stein

Traders can cause short-term volatility. In the long run, the market must revert to a sensible price/earnings multiple.

Ben Stein

Trying to pick individual stocks is a trap. I can't do it. Warren Buffett can, but hardly anyone else can beat the indexes over a long period of time.

Ben Stein

Usually I am not a conspiracy theorist. I don't believe in the Bilderbergers as a conspiracy or the Trilateralists. But I am certain that the Communists killed JFK. There is a super great book called 'Legend' by Edward Jay Epstein that makes it all perfectly clear.

Ben Stein

We are not supposed to be all equal. Let's just forget that. We are supposed to have equal rights under law. If we do that, we have done enough.

Ben Stein

We in the media are just people with all of people's faults.

Ben Stein

We're a lazy, undisciplined generation. I don't exempt myself: I spend way too much, even though I make a good income.

Ben Stein

When Hollywood sees a good story about a man who sells confidence, they see themselves and they like it.

Ben Stein

When I seemed to be irritable or sad, my father would quote the learned Dr. Knight, and then say, 'Just go to sleep.' Like all smart aleck kids, I thought the advice was silly. But as I've grown older, I've realized just how smart Knight was.

Ben Stein

When are American Jews going to realize that the Republican Party is far better for Israel than the Democrats?

Ben Stein

Wow, bad news. Mr. Obama now hates Israel because the Israelis want to build 1,600 apartments in their own capital city, Jerusalem. Russia hates Israel, too. So do the Europeans. So does Ban Ki-moon, a Korean who is secretary-general of the UN.

Ben Stein

Yes, Americans can still get credit for cars and trucks and refrigerators, and those businesses are doing well. But just try to get a home loan now.

Ben Stein

You cannot win if you're not at the table. You have to be where the action is.

Ben Stein

You must take the first step. The first steps will take some effort, maybe pain. But after that, everything that has to be done is real-life movement.

Ben Stein

This page is intentionally left blank

This page is intentionally left blank

This page is intentionally left blank

This page is intentionally left blank

This page is intentionally left blank